House

House

Myra Connell

Nine
Arches
Press

House
Myra Connell

ISBN: 978-0-9931201-4-5

First published September 2015 by:

Nine Arches Press
PO Box 6269
Rugby
CV21 9NL
United Kingdom

www.ninearchespress.com

Printed in Britain by:
The Russell Press Ltd.

Contents

THREE

For JS

ONE

One

So here's the house.
It makes the corner,
stands where two streets meet,
and looks towards the sea.
One flat wave is foaming at the kerb,
the water green, and icy.

The tide is at the door,
and yet the woman says it isn't high enough for bathing.
That's a lie: she lied,
the woman with the black and shining hair,
to stop the other swimming.

Out the window to the sea-front
they could see the waves run in
slant and slant against the road.
She lied.
Or both the women lied,
needing one the other.

I want to know more about these cows

Mornings, they're out: big bodies,
roan, cream, and grey with mottles. Heavy, nose to nose.
Steam rises from their nostrils, backs.

This triangle of grass and mud (*a pretty triangle*, she said)
is bordered by a stream, which they could cross,
the cows, by sliding down the pock-marked bank
and wading. Beyond, a meadow.

By noon, he's locked them in again.
The black shed doors are closed, three hay-rolls
rustler-stacked against them. Inside
the cows are back in fetid darkness.

He himself has gone to early dinner,
sleeping in his chair.

To J

Last night we went to find wood, too mean to buy for the fire
pine chunks bagged in orange, kindling. Found a track,
past a lodge or gatehouse, beech trees. No-one there.
No dog barked. No light shone, although a car was parked.

Snapped branches with our feet, broke sticks; left piles beside
    the road.
And then a bridge of rusty iron; and past a cattle-grid,
a field of bullocks. The youngest stared us out, the others fled.
Undaunted, though they'd gathered on the ridge above the path,

you led us off again and round to where they waited.
You growled, *harrumphed,* and batted on your leg the map
to keep them back. Another bridge, planks rotten,
and the track was overgrown; another silent house,

dark path, the road. A field of turnips under fleece.
No-one stopped us. Didn't need to wish the engine silent,
taking from the verge our piles of wood.

Whiteadder, Monday evening

Relationships are often constituted by what one dare not say to the other person. – Adam Phillips

A man was up there burning something. The air was acrid,
then we saw the smoke. If we were in love, it would be fine
to hide like this; for something to have come upon me. So,
one could account for it: the lying low, not speaking.

A pump was taking water from the river,
or pumping something in. Flat, flood-plain wheat-field,
half-moon-shaped, at dusk. The tractor-tracks were deeper,
black, because the soil was sodden.

And then he'd gone, the man, although the gate stood open.
Don't go looking. It's evidence he's been burning.
Don't go further up the path, in case.

There's something. I have lost my sense of smell.
I am afraid I'll kill you. So far?
No. I haven't.

On Arran

1.

Someone had lived there, in that pile of stones,
the orange lilies showed it. Later, in the book I read his name:
Jimmy Neil, the whelkman. His wife was Jennie.
They had come from Campbeltown by boat,
attracted by the wave-made harbour: cleft in rock,
with jellyfish today – three fierce purple, one a rusty star.
And there they built the house, of stones,
with heather for the roof. They both collected whelks.
She took them every Monday in a bag
and left it on the road to Drumadoon.

2.

I am swinging from the ladder, star-splayed;
I stepped wrong-footed; dangle.
There was a sound that had to come; and though at night
I'd loved you, in the morning I drew back.

3.

Now, rain. Three days' downpour, and the names of dyes:
Weld with Alum Mordant. Bracken Tips,
and Cochineal, and Lichen (from both wood and stone).
Onion Skin, Bog Myrtle. Otherwise, the rain;
the need to raise the spirits, air the coats.
Children peer from fogged-up windows. We crack
and use the heating, standing by the meter counting.
Nothing dries. No wind, and air that's turned to water.
Even the seals
no longer lollop to the rock to bask.

Sorry for your loss

1.

Is there something in the dreams? *Lettuces*, you said.
But that's not much. Can't live on lettuce.
The van drawn up, and then the woman, stooped,
who keeps her witch-eye on the ground,
talking on the doorstep as I stood there tea in hand,
refusing to invite her in.

The thought that all was lost, which meant:
You're not so special after all you know.
And standing like a victim as the tannin stains my teeth,
the smell of milk disgusts me.

Her husband died. Do those girls, her neighbours,
fear her? As we feared Henny-Henny,
and the woman with the hats?
She also lived alone, had grey net curtains
and some once-white with prints of roses
that were always closed. She too was bent,
looked up only from one slant eye's edge.

2.

Each day they go out smiling. Drive a little car in eau-de-nil.
She has changed from blonde to brown,
today wears ballet shoes and stirrup-pants, and he
checked shirt and glasses.

3.

"For the boys," she said, the lank grey hair, the kirby-grips,
"I must be strong." I fear her; fear her need,
her madness. Like her, I want a fortress now,
a barricade.

Imagine

          if ease could be possible
here in this sweet place where –

neither of us speaks.
Let's go to Galloway,

to the dark-park there,
to see the stars.

My heart is bruised. I lay at night
and felt it creaking. Now

the car-alarm, the hunger.
An open plastic sack. Someone banging nails.

The clock.

441 267

1.

The roofs are falling in, we see it from the road.
The shops are gone: the Gainsborough,
Arcadia, Coffey's butcher, the fruiterer Mulholland.
There's an empty space there, sky, where slates
have slipped. Her house, my mother's,
will be standing by a city interchange.

2.

Behind the pub, the railway line, the mountain.
Look up the road.
There's the corner-house, already ruined,
the mad old lady (they say the rats have had her cash),
and now the other roofs are gapped.

Everyone has left: Bunchie, Mamie, Mike the dog;
the Cuthberts with their green gate; Norman,
all the ones between, they've gone, and there's her house,
and she alone. Big old house.
Something encroaching like the tide.

Vein

The Tigris and Euphrates, forking.
Humped, a range of mountains.
Nothing is enough, except today, for moments,
sky's enough, and wind. The shadow.
Here, with butterfly, some lace, the beech-tree speaking,
perhaps a restoration. Peeled paint, long grass,
the money for the scaffold.

All in one day, it came to me.
I was taken over, something speaking through me.
Rain again tomorrow. The river swelling.
People, farms, the fields of wheat
are drowned.

We stood there on the windy island gazing at the sea,
while rolled-up-trousered men, and boys with buckets
trawled pools, called, "Crab!" across the sand, and,
"Look!"

The knuckle-hills. Stretched dead toad,
silver, to be fitted in the silver tin. You are fooling us.
You're leading us astray. Your words are nothing, play.
Want echo, want the cutting back; remember
just the toad, the pencil-case we found beside the road.
Hot sun beating, for which we had a scarf in blue.
What is this *blue*? Blue like sky,
blue like the butterfly, like denim, like your eyes.
Certain pots are blue.
The Tigris?

Beyond Llandudno

1.

The last farm, rotting. Humans hide indoors,
and in the byre hock-deep, heifers, slurry.
Voices to-fro murmur. A door upstairs,
a footstep on a creaking board, a woman singing.

Something, you said, is elemental:
sea, the cottages, the cliffs; the starlings
flocking from the hinterland at dusk
to pier-roost on the metal struts.
This old stone house against the sea;
the empty grate.

2.

And sunk in dampness.
Someone, over years, had scraped together dykes
and dug a ditch for drainage. Someone bulldozed here
the roots of willows, sprouting now again,
as flood-defence. Propped two great tractor-wheels
against the rusted iron barn, and piles of birch-wood,
mossed.

3.

Across the path, an arch of thorn-trees,
berried now, and leaning in.
He planted them for her, and led her,
newly wed, to that hard life.

Sheep on the hillside. Unfenced cliff.
The dog, the hens, the muddy yard.
No steps cut to reach the sea,
and to the neighbours the long field walk;
big house, deferential.

Bridal arch. The ache. Whin (one burnt to black)
and battered thorns against the hill.
That blank grate. The bedroom where he loved her,
where the child was born, has fallen in. Is left,
without comment, in the darkness, shut.

After Medard Boss's description
of schizophrenia

A chair there was, and on it I must sit,
because it stood there. It invited,
it commanded, me. (Here's the rubbish-man,
on time, coming through the train.
Put in his plastic bag your empty cup,
and thank him.)

What is the meaning of that mark on the wall?
I must know everything about it, I must not walk on
until I find who put it there, and why, and what to say.
And then the origin of life; and after that the wine-glass,
the little one engraved and dipped in green,
the one I used at mother's. Where is it now?
Can I find it, can I dowse it in the universe,
in the zillion houses, somewhere through the walls?
Or in the sitting-rooms, the cupboards like the one she
        kept it in?

These things call me. They *insist*.
That man gardening, over there – bending by the rosebed,
clearing with his gloved hands last year's leaves –
I stand here open mouthed,
he swallows me.
All I can be is him.

He is burning something in an oil-drum.
Smoke blows
across the road,
across the backs of cattle huddled there.

TWO

Bring me

1.

Bring me salad, salsify; bring chicory;
bring apple-juice in flagons. Pick for me
blackberries, the last ones, fly-blown,
and leave them standing
so the silver maggot-snakes rear up
for picking out with tweezers.

2.

We peeled potatoes, he and I,
which though washed were earthy.
We had two bottles of Moselle.
He seemed content to marry me.

Emulsion

As if that was the only way to have the room:
the door, the chair, the couch like that,
the way the sun comes in.
As if a window-sill with pigeons,
the soffits flaking, light just so,
were needed for the cure,
and I must make my home the same.

Here. Two floors up. The chimney wind,
the magpies.
Cloud and scratching sky, the willow;
summer heat, the draughts in March.
Does the brightness –
does the rising up to heaven –
does walking through the house mean something,
and being here alone?

Is the white too stark, the blue too like the sky?
Is the journey up the stairs too long?

Will there be space to hide?

For – , beginning.

It's dark, and may be not a crossing
but a journey all in darkness: a wandering, a being lost
in only dark, not know, and end in darkness too.

Allow the small thing. Let me allow you, small thing,
let you be. Something not yet come to birth;
perhaps not yet implanted.

If I could come –
if I could come to you more certain. If I could welcome –
find a welcome for you. Well come, with your fear.

Consulting room

Here's the mausoleum. Here's the seagull
that she brought from Heipertz.
Here's the barometer her father chose, in walnut;
the Raymond Piper portrait.

Not about the seagull (which she loved,
which made her think of home)
and not about the cellar or the jars of jam and plums,
there is a secret: something whispered. 'Of course,
we didn't care for him.' 'We never liked that man.'
'She would have him, though we told her no.'

Later, when she sighed, and slept alone,
and when her mouth set downwards,
she didn't tell them, out of pride.
It's susurrated, whispered, sybillation, shhh.

Shall we have the German art, gilt-framed; the mirror?
What about the curtains, will I change them every May?
Will I have a curtain for the door, and close it,
slowly, as I let you in?

And the rooms behind, neglected.
This is one of them. We are going to this room to work.
We are walking down towards it, we have turned.
We look.

Landslide

1.

I carry water in a cup,
alone and careful.
Careful careful.

It is bulging up
the water in the cup.
It's standing proud

for you
who light my life.
I mustn't spill it.

I am charged with it
as charged the world is
with God's grandeur,

which flames out,
shines. Light of the world,
I will light your life too.

Let me.
Let me be your beacon
light your life.

2.

She is carrying a cup
she hardly dares to step (oh, sleep).

Not one drop must be spilled –
and look, it isn't drops, it's thicker,

it's a solid thing this water, how it
bulges on the surface.

It wouldn't be a drop that fell.
A sheet perhaps.

A torrent.

Two

It was a brick house, ugly, in suburbs out of town –
Solihull perhaps, the green-signed lanes of Lapworth,
    Hockley Heath.
In front, a swimming-pool, thick with weed and algae;
a wall beside it, sodden blinds.

Someone would have bought it, there was money to be made.
The agent shook his head. Beat him, he said,
why someone should forget they owned it.
Place like that. An asset.

Who is the person who forgot?
She's distracted, lives elsewhere.
She has another life. You could say
she doesn't pay attention, you could say she's mad.

I confirm there is nothing

The two rooms are empty.
The plate from last night's dinner
stands on the floor outside.

But we look clear-eyed at emptiness,
are learning not to fear it;
or impotence, or barren fields,

cracked clay below thin wheat,
the horse disconsolate.

Here is bareness.
Here is space.
Here quiet.

China Seagull

It is smooth like skin but cold,
and when I lick it it tastes like salt.
(We must be careful at all times and know what we want.)
When I see it, I think of my grandmother.
I think of her house

and the cellar with the jars of jam,
and the garden, and the orchard, and the blackbirds
in summer in the cherry-tree by the wall.
It is smooth like skin but cold
and when I lick it it tastes like salt.

We must be careful and at all times know what we want;
but the seagull is smooth to the touch and cool,
and I think of my grandmother
and her fingers which were bent, and which plaited
each morning the long hair of her daughters.

And I think of her house with its cellar
and the jars of jam and preserves,
and of the orchard, and her hands stained with beetroot.
My seagull is smooth like skin.
When I lick it it reminds me of salt

and of the blackbird, this last summer, in the tree by the wall.

She opened the glass door

1.

There was too much of Lvov, and Queen Anne cherries,
sunlight. When you had packed, were ready,
when the aunties, clean and starched,
sent servants wearing aprons quickly to fetch cream,
when the morning waited, wanting you to leave –

2.

Each day at dawn she checked the mountains:
if they gave themselves today or hid;
were blue, or if the sun had turned them pink.
(Cream. Bring cream.) And drank for breakfast,
for her heart, a schnapps. Station, porters, salamanders.

The trees were lances, poplars set in rows.
Dew had made a suitcase wet,
from which we knew it had been left all night
out by the pebbled wall:
now, early morning, drying in the sun.

3.

And Anton: when any woman passed he raised his shirt
to show the chest-to-navel scar. He'd lost his spleen,
in Spain, in eighty-three; and now his memory was gone.
He had a notebook where he wrote the names.

His scissors cut the town, Carpathian,
cut borders, suburbs. Soft Lvov
with ships at harbour; boulders; water-breaks;
the men at prayer.

Written after reading *To go to Lvov* by Adam Zagajewski

Button Tie

And one light on, a naked bulb, and later, smoke,
and in a net, nuts for blue-tits. Granny's house.
A scattering outside of new-split logs, left
where the rain will get them. The button on the mattress.
Old bed, in darkness. Deed of darkness.

I see her, walking fast across the green, barefaced,
laughing with a red-haired youth: as if they have escaped
and she is free – from lipstick, earrings, home.
And then her car, lights on, parked outside.
He is driving. I think of turning back.

There's a second's pause –
and in that second, what? A gathering of parcels, a finishing?
A kiss? For her to tell him something so compelling
that it cannot wait? He shepherds her, as men do women.
She bows her head, and takes her long black coat inside.

They are inspecting the fruit trees in the corner field.
A van, a yellow car, are parked between the rows,
doors open. Men are looking at the buds
to see if, tempted by the short mild winter,
they've been damaged by the last days' frost;
if their tips are blackened;
what harvest is to come.

THREE

Escape

1.

A sea-light in the room. I find a book she's reading,
stone-blue cover, flowered, slightly torn,
the page turned over where she left it.

I see her sandy tan. Her clothes are bleached.
Her son is here, and drunk, and lurches in;
he tells me I must leave a note.

2.

Squeezed by the fear of dying,
I want to run away.
There's sun on Friday. Southwold.

3.

Two round stones from Arran, from the beach at Shiskine,
weight the corners of the yard;
hold me down like ballast.

All this rain

She thanked me when I left

Keep hold of me, I said

The ghost is here

The sudden closing of the heart

the rain.

Lexical (I)

Do you love me enough not to mind?
Oh yes, I love you, yes, love;
and look away, and so I've lost it, lost
something again that mattered.

You can put me out, it's fine;
can't put out my fire. That little book
you lent me, I refused it.
Too hot, take it back.

I couldn't (words, their opposites:
I so much want to)
read it, I would have had to wrap it,
make a cover; put it on the mantelpiece

beside the bottle-ship, the soapstone cat;
or lay it on the altar. Besides – a dictionary –
why *borrow* one of those?
You were silent, in your orange shirt,

or *blouse* we used to say. Blowsy,
blown, your bedroom eyes.
Somehow to escape, to find a garden
with a fence, the dogs kept out.

Lexical (II)

Now there's new beech.
Water cleanses, just a rinse, a dip.
Two drops upon a baby's head,
and dunk the spinach. Eleven plus

examined brains not cleanliness,
and so they came the Fane Street kids,
were clever but neglected, smelled,
had impetigo. The professor's children got it,

the mothers grumbled over folded arms.

To X

I thought I heard your footstep on the stairs.
Remembered then those plane leaves, brown,
I'd seen them blown there. They made the sound.

Earlier, at dusk, a robin sang. Now
the sound of helicopters, sirens, as if the city's up in flames.
I don't know where you are. I'm afraid I've broken you,

and now you've stayed away. You've left no word.
It's late, you won't come now. I'm sorry.
I will miss you. Miss you now.

What Angel Would Hear Me?

(after reading Jessica Benjamin.)

I must become a Mary dressed in blue,
with babies at the breast and halo;
pair of babies, twins who –

                    in this first gaze, the beauty,
and the thing that leaves (new leaves, beech, their softness),
the thing impossible to influence will leave, or die.

They slam you cold upon the metal scales.
At once you'll be discovered
good or lacking; fat or underweight, defective.
Leave you then to work it out alone,
to manage somehow.

And a crossing of the water, where the fret is smoothed.
A ring of water round an island.
Children jumping in and splashing, shouting.
May: as if it's only clouds that matter
and the fear that now I've said, I've entered into you.
I have come into the room and dream about your body
    holding me,
your hands on mine.

Just Peachy

1.

This winter I will fix the vine securely to the fence.
Lift stems, screw in hooks, stretch green wire.

2.

A man is in the house, disturbs me.
Give me my beauty back,
my face.

3.

A grey car was in her drive one day.
Someone came to feed the cat. The lights went on.

When she returns the roses will have blown,
sweet peas gone grey with mould, and in the drive
they'll find the yellow seeds of plane-trees, leaves.

She will be wearing gold and cashmere,

I scratch in heavy wool. She smiles.
Her husband wears an overcoat and doesn't smell.
I dream she is an addict. I would like to think –

but I am muffled: bundled like faggots,
like a pump in winter wrapped in sacking.
I am lagged against the frost.

I have ploughed on, through cold and dirt.
I have faced the greasy stove,
the make-do; things without a shine.

Does she too feel the heavy sky,
the mustard-yellow cloud,
the damp? Has she almost drowned?

Wolf Man

The pantry door was open. Outside, sounds of shouting,
dogs; and in the night a man was falling.

The dog was baying, starved.
I saw it grab his arm. I saw his face,
unshaven.

A man, a wolf, has left his slippers by the stairs,
has gone into the larder.

After Walter Benjamin

We had to find out about the town he came from:

about the streets, the sewers; the script the council chose

for the plaques and signs; the corner-shops: who ran them,

when they closed at night. We needed more about his house

and where his mother hung the bedding in the mornings.

Only knowing this, we thought, we'd understand him;

explain the warehouse with its dusty silks, and then at last

the need he had to clear it: paying, through the nose, for
    that long skip.

Three

1.

Who is this agent?
If he'd had a house like this
he would not have let it rot.

He would have cleaned the pool,
used chemicals to kill the weed.
It was an asset,
but it's gone to waste.

2.

She's been somewhere else.
She's been walking in the woods perhaps;
hiding;
hoping she will not be found.

Sitting on orange boxes, 4 a.m.

and drinking tea with Coffee Mate
from cups the builders left,
we held on until the end. I held, that is,

to you. I don't know if you held me.
Now I feel my bones becoming lighter,
the muscle fall away, the skin too big.

I knew that she was ill, Kat said.
I watched her getting smaller;
and somehow that is me, that dwindle.

I didn't know the will to live would be so lacking,
the will to die so lively
when we left.

At this corner

there has been a fire. There is charcoal, ash,
there's broken glass. Awake again, I feel it in the heart.

Sometimes I can think of other things:
the horses near the roundabout; perhaps a trip, the coast. Now

what I feel is tired, knowing I must learn to live without you.

Someone will read it all

                              and find the meaning
but it won't be me. I feel too much like sleep;
and with the kitten, with the sense of outrage,
and the roaring of the plane – something speaks –
remembering the candy-floss, the pier –
says something quiet, something easily dismissed.

It is easy, once again, to make the episodes important:
the half-ditch; the dusty hole beside the road
where branches from an oak dried out for firewood.
You lit the stove. I squatted there to watch the water boil.
Tinder, kindling; the cross-roads where the bottles –
woman at the window. Three men came inside;
and out there on the hillside,
storms.

Things are too sharp

I doubt if I dare go out now in this coat of sleep;
something fast will hit me on the High Street
crossing from Boots to Juicy Fruits: bicycles, perambulators,
push-chairs. If someone offered me his arm –
my son perhaps – or held my hand;
took me to the Prince's garden in the sun
and bought me Guinness –

Will someone shelter me – someone say I needn't –
someone like the tall young man
who takes the lady in her purple coat,
daily to the post-box?

Can I have a window facing south,
a patch of green? Go quiet; listen;
watch with gentle eyes?

He turned and looked at me today.
He was standing by the gate. A frost.
The cows inside again,
the yard a lake.

Acknowledgements

In 'Landslide', the lines 'I am charged with it / as charged the world is / with God's grandeur, / which flames out, / shines' echo the lines from Gerald Manley Hopkins' poem 'God's Grandeur': 'The world is charged with the grandeur of God. / It will flame out, like shining from shook foil.'

These poems have come from years of friendship, writing and conversation with David Hart. He has read them all in some form, and our thinking together about language and poetry continues to matter very much to me.

I am grateful to Jane Commane for her skill and patience as an editor.